Lessons on Demand I

Teacher Guide and Novel Unit for The Inquisitor's Tale

By:
John Pennington

The lessons on demand series is designed to provide ready to use resources for novel study. In this book you will find key vocabulary, student organizer pages, and assessments. This guide is divided into two sections. Section one is the teacher section which consists of vocabulary and activities. Section two holds all of the student pages, including assessments and graphic organizers.

Now available! Student Workbooks!

Find them on Amazon.com

Other titles include...

The War That Saved My Life

Esperanza Rising

Walk Two Moons

The Giver

One Crazy Summer

The One and Only Ivan

Flora & Ulysses

Island of the Blue Dolphin

The Little Prince

The Lightning Thief

Where the Red Fern Grows

And more........

Section One

- Teacher Pages
- Vocabulary
- Suggested Activities

NAME:

TEACHER:

Date:

Chapters 1-6 Vocabulary

Venerate

Heresy

Pagan

Retinue

Procession

Blasphemy

Oblate

Theology

Pious

Penance

Superstition

Empathetic

Chapters 1-6 Activities

<u>Reading Check Question / Quiz:</u>

What ability does Jeanna have? She can see the future.

What is William like? Large, dark skinned, strong.

What special skill does Jacob have? He can heal and is intelligent.

What happens to Gwenforte? Is killed after protecting Jeanns and then returns years later.

<u>Blooms Higher Order Question:</u>

Diagram all special, beyond worldly, actions demonstrated by characters in the story.

<u>Suggested Activity Sheets (see Section Two):</u>

Character Sketch—Jeanna

Character Sketch—William

Character Sketch—Jacob

Research Connection—Aristotle

Draw the Scene

Who, What, When, Where and How

<u>Discussion Questions</u>

What do you think Jeanna's life would have been like if she had not had the visions?

What are all of the injustices that William hears and experiences?

Why do you think Jacob's parents did not confront the Christian boy?

Are the children saints? Why?

NAME:

TEACHER:

Date:

Chapters 7-14 Vocabulary

Elaborating

Paranoid

Cacophonous

Envy

Liberate

Crenellations

Pungent

Flatulence

Petition

Grievance

Vassal

Verdict

Chapters 7-14 Activities

<u>Reading Check Question / Quiz:</u>

What is William allowed to fight with? Flesh and Bone

Why is the dragon dangerous? Flammable flatulence

What diagnosis does Jacob arrive at to cure the dragon? It is allergic to cheese and feeds it a cure.

Who arrives to rescue Jeanna and Jacob after they are no longer in danger? William and Gwenforte

<u>Blooms Higher Order Question:</u>

Design your own group of saints and describe what miracles they would preform.

<u>Suggested Activity Sheets (see Section Two):</u>

Character Sketch—Sir Fabian

Character Sketch—Marmeluc

Character Sketch—Lord Bertulf

Research Connection—Damascus

Research Connection—The Crusades

Precognition Sheet

What Would You Do?

<u>Discussion Questions</u>

What makes someone a saint?

Do you think any of the children are saints? Why?

Could a religious war like the crusades happen again? Support your opinion.

NAME:	TEACHER:
	Date:

Chapters 14-27 Vocabulary

Deceive

Iota

Banality

Desecrate

Advocate

Ostentatious

Usurious

Valet

Revelry

Piebald

Charade

Martyrdom

Chapters 14-27 Activities

Reading Check Question / Quiz:

What are the children trying to prevent the King of France from doing? Burning the Hebrew / Jewish books.

What keeps Jeanna from acting on the plan to have a visions and fit for the king? Jacob confronts them about the burning before she has a chance.

Where do the children find a Hebrew book they can save? Back with Williams donkey at the inn.

Who do they meet again at the abbey they never expected to see again? Michelangelo de Bologna

Blooms Higher Order Question:

Consider new chapter titles for the 27 chapters. List the new chapter title and what happens in the chapter that supports your new title.

Suggested Activity Sheets (see Section Two):

Character Sketch—Michelangelo de Bologna

Character Sketch—King of France

Character Sketch—Blanche de Castile

Character Sketch—Etienne d'Anles

Research Connection—Notre Dame

Create the Test

Interview

Top Ten List—Events

Write a Letter

NAME:

TEACHER:

Date:

Chapter Vocabulary

Chapter Activities

Reading Check Question / Quiz:

Blooms Higher Order Question:

Suggested Activity Sheets (see Section Two):

Discussion Questions

NAME:
TEACHER:
Date:

Chapter Vocabulary

Chapter Activities

Reading Check Question / Quiz:

Blooms Higher Order Question:

Suggested Activity Sheets (see Section Two):

Discussion Questions

Section Two

Student Work Pages

Work Pages

Graphic Organizers

Assessments

Activity Descriptions

Advertisement—Select an item from the text and have the students use text clues to draw an advertisement about that item.

Chapter to Poem—Students select 20 words from the text to write a five line poem with 3 words on each line.

Character Sketch—Students complete the information about a character using text clues.

Comic Strip— Students will create a visual representation of the chapter in a series of drawings.

Compare and Contrast—Select two items to make relationship connections with text support.

Create the Test—have the students use the text to create appropriate test questions.

Draw the Scene—students use text clues to draw a visual representation of the chapter.

Interview— Students design questions you would ask a character in the book and then write that characters response.

Lost Scene—Students use text clues to decide what would happen after a certain place in the story.

Making Connections—students use the text to find two items that are connected and label what kind of relationship connects them.

Precognition Sheet—students envision a character, think about what will happen next, and then determine what the result of that would be.

Activity Descriptions

Pyramid—Students use the text to arrange a series of items in an hierarchy format.

Research Connection—Students use an outside source to learn more about a topic in the text.

Sequencing—students will arrange events in the text in order given a specific context.

Support This! - Students use text to support a specific idea or concept.

Travel Brochure—Students use information in the text to create an informational text about the location

Top Ten List—Students create a list of items ranked from 1 to 10 with a specific theme.

Vocabulary Box—Students explore certain vocabulary words used in the text.

What Would You Do? - Students compare how characters in the text would react and compare that with how they personally would react.

Who, What, When, Where, and How—Students create a series of questions that begin with the following words that are connected to the text.

Write a Letter—Students write a letter to a character in the text.

Activity Descriptions (for scripts and poems)

Add a Character—Students will add a character that does not appear in the scene and create dialog and responses from other characters.

Costume Design—Students will design costumes that are appropriate to the characters in the scene and explain why they chose the design.

Props Needed— Students will make a list of props they believe are needed and justify their choices with text.

Soundtrack! - Students will create a sound track they believe fits the play and justify each song choice.

Stage Directions— Students will decide how the characters should move on, around, or off stage.

Poetry Analysis—Students will determine the plot, theme, setting, subject, tone and important words and phrases.

NAME: TEACHER:

Date:

Advertisement: Draw an advertisement for _____

NAME:

TEACHER:

Date:

Chapter to Poem

Assignment: Select 20 words found in the chapter to create a poem where each line is 3 words long.

Title:

NAME: TEACHER: Date:

Character Sketch

Name

Draw a picture

Personality/ Distinguishing marks

Connections to other characters

Important Actions

NAME:

TEACHER:

Date:

Comic Strip

NAME:

TEACHER:

Date:

Compare and Contrast Venn Diagram

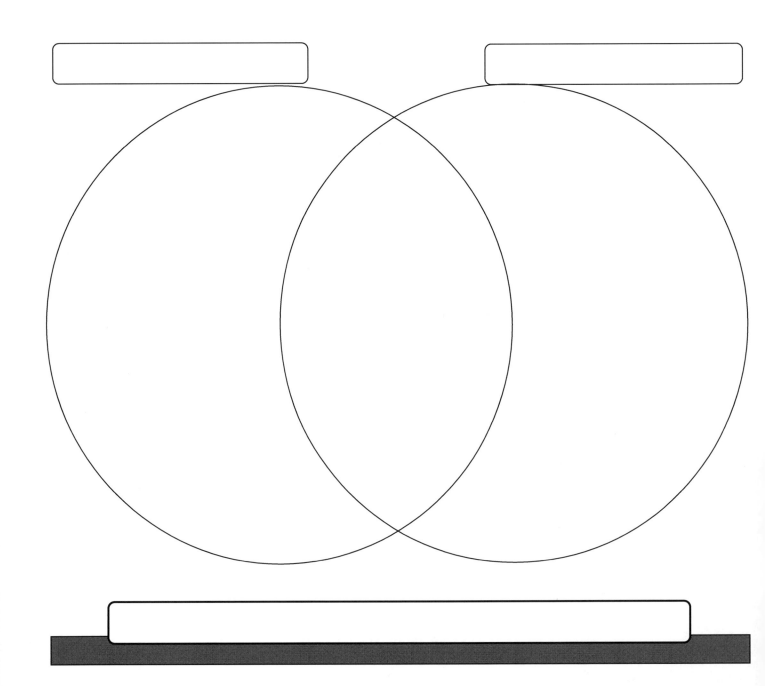

NAME:

TEACHER:

Date:

Create the Test

Question:

Answer:

Question:

Answer:

Question:

Answer:

Question:

Answer:

NAME:

TEACHER:

Date:

Draw the Scene: What five things have you included in the scene?

1

2

3

4

5

NAME:

TEACHER:

Date:

Interview: Who _____

Question:

Answer:

Question:

Answer:

Question:

Answer:

Question:

Answer:

NAME:

TEACHER:

Date:

Lost Scene: Write a scene that takes place between _____ and _____

NAME:

TEACHER:

Date:

Making Connections

What is the connection?

NAME:

TEACHER:

Date:

Precognition Sheet

Who ?

What's going to happen?

What will be the result?

Who ?

What's going to happen?

What will be the result?

Who ?

What's going to happen?

What will be the result?

Who ?

What's going to happen?

What will be the result?

How many did you get correct?

NAME:

TEACHER:

Date:

Assignment: Pyramid

NAME:

TEACHER:

Date:

Research connections

Source (URL, Book, Magazine, Interview)

What am I researching?

Facts I found that could be useful or notes

1.

2.

3.

4.

5.

6.

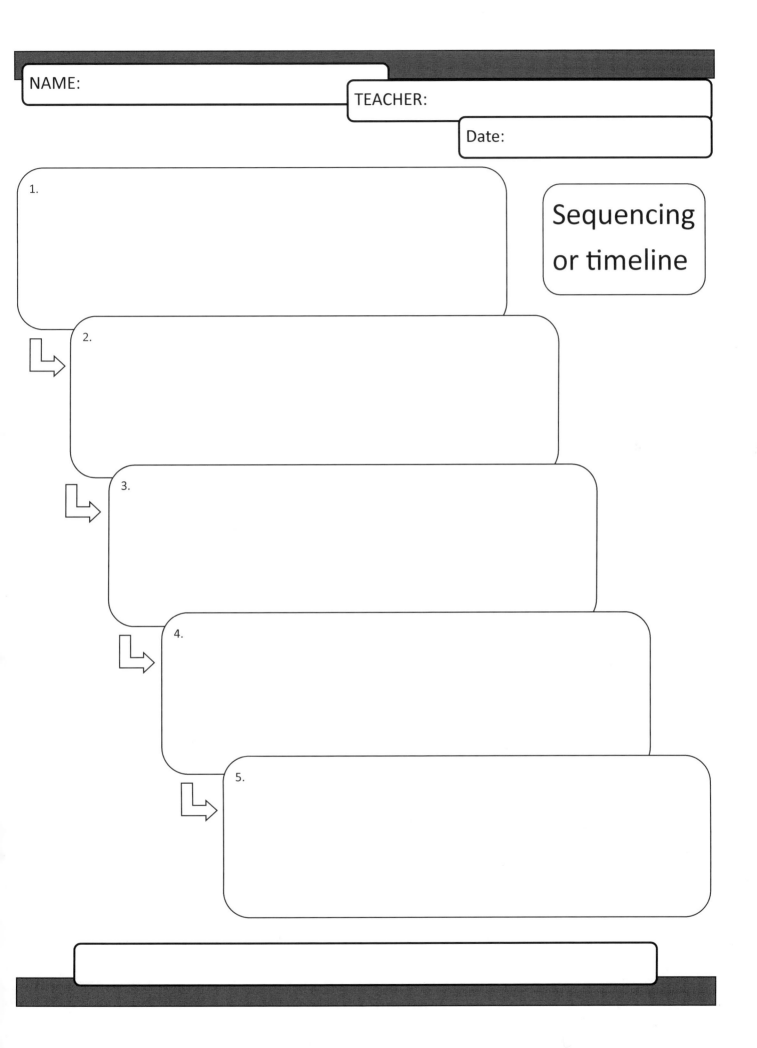

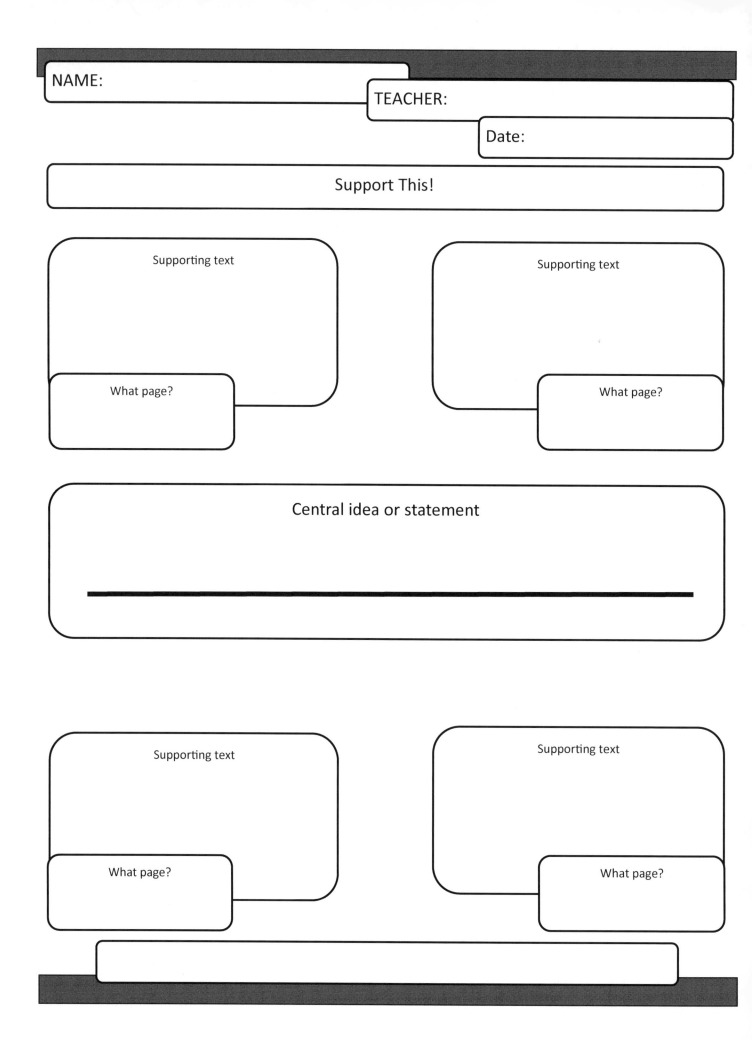

NAME:

TEACHER:

Date:

Travel Brochure

Why should you visit?

What are you going to see?

Map

Special Events

NAME:

TEACHER:

Date:

Top Ten List

1.
2.
3.
4.
5.
6.
7.
8.
9.
10.

NAME:

TEACHER:

Date:

Vocabulary Box

Definition:

Draw:

Word:

Related words:

Use in a sentence:

Definition:

Draw:

Word:

Related words:

Use in a sentence:

NAME:

TEACHER:

Date:

What would you do?

Character: _____

What did they do?

Example from text:

What would you do?

Why would that be better?

Character: _____

What did they do?

Example from text:

What would you do?

Why would that be better?

Character: _____

What did they do?

Example from text:

What would you do?

Why would that be better?

NAME:

TEACHER:

Date:

Who, What, When, Where, and How

Who

What

Where

When

How

NAME:

TEACHER:

Date:

Write a letter

To:

From:

NAME:

TEACHER:

Date:

Assignment:

NAME:

TEACHER:

Date:

Add a Character

Who is the new character?

What reason does the new character have for being there?

Write a dialog between the new character and characters currently in the scene.

You dialog must be 6 lines or more, and can occur in the beginning, middle or end of the scene.

NAME:

TEACHER:

Date:

Costume Design

Draw a costume for one the characters in the scene.

Why do you believe this character should have a costume like this?

NAME:

TEACHER:

Date:

Props Needed

Prop:

What text from the scene supports this?

Prop:

What text from the scene supports this?

Prop:

What text from the scene supports this?

NAME:

TEACHER:

Date:

Soundtrack!

Song:

Why should this song be used?

Song:

Why should this song be used?

Song:

Why should this song be used?

NAME:

TEACHER:

Date:

Stage Directions

List who is moving, how they are moving and use text from the dialog to determine when they move.

Who:

How:

When:

Who:

How:

When:

Who:

How:

When:

NAME:

TEACHER:

Poetry Analysis

Date:

Name of Poem:

Subject:
- Text Support:

Plot:
- Text Support:

Theme:
- Text Support:

Setting:
- Text Support:

Tone:
- Text Support:

Important Words and Phrases:

Why are these words and phrases important:

Made in the USA
Columbia, SC
02 October 2017